First published by Parragon in 2011

Parragon
Queen Street House
4 Queen Street
Bath BA1 1HE, UK

All information correct as of January 2011

ISBN: 978-1-4454-4111-5

Manufactured in China

FOOTBALL FILE

Parragon

Bath • New York • Singapore • Hong Kong • Cologne • Delhi
Melbourne • Amsterdam • Johannesburg • Auckland • Shenzhen

CONTENTS

INTRODUCTION

Welcome to your very own Football File! A must-read collection of facts, stats and info about some of the best players in the world. Check out details on Europe's top clubs and test your footy knowledge with some testing and fun activities. Enjoy the cool and comprehensive player profiles, select your dream team and never miss a game again by filling in your own fixture list and calendar.

PLAYER PROFILES

Check out the profiles of some of the best players in the world. Then fill in profiles of your favourite players and complete your own details too.

Name: Lionel Messi
One of the most naturally talented players on the planet, the hugely entertaining Argentine star possesses fantastic pace, balance and close control of the ball, which allows him to dribble past markers for fun. Messi also has the ability to score goals from all distances and angles.
Position: Winger, Attacking midfielder
Born: 24 June, 1987 in Rosario, Argentina
Height: 5 ft 7 in (1.69 m)
Club: Barcelona
Former clubs: None
Shirt number: 10
International team: Argentina
Achievements: La Liga winner, Champions League winner, Olympic Gold Medallist

Did you know?

Lionel claimed the 2009/10 European Golden Shoe award after netting 34 times in La Liga and finishing as Europe's top goalscorer that season.

Team-mates

Use this space to add some of this player's top team-mates for both club and country.

Scouting Report

Write a list of this player's greatest skills to complete a detailed scouting report.

Name: Cristiano Ronaldo

King of the stepover, Cristiano Ronaldo is one of the most dangerous attacking talents around. His ability to perform breathtaking skills at breakneck speed makes him a defender's nightmare. A free-kick expert who scores goals for fun, the Real Madrid star is a class act.

Position: Winger, Forward

Born: 5 February, 1985 in Madeira, Portugal

Height: 6 ft 1 in (1.85 m)

Club: Real Madrid

Former clubs: Sporting Lisbon, Manchester United

Shirt number: 7

International team: Portugal

Achievements: Three-time FA Premier League champion, Champions League winner, FIFA World Player of the Year in 2008

Did you know?

When Cristiano Ronaldo joined Real Madrid from Manchester United in 2009, he became the world's most expensive footballer. The Spanish giants paid a record £80m for the Portuguese star.

Team-mates

Use this space to add some of this player's top team-mates for both club and country.

____

____

____

Scouting Report

Write a list of this player's greatest skills to complete a detailed scouting report.

____

____

____

____

____

Name: Wayne Rooney

The English striker uses his physical strength and great hunger and desire for the game to maximize his displays for both club and country. An excellent finisher, Rooney's movement off the ball makes him extremely difficult to mark. He is already established as one of the world's finest, but is still improving season by season.

Position: Striker

Born: 24 October, 1985 in Liverpool, England

Height: 5 ft 10 in (1.78 m)

Club: Manchester United

Former clubs: Everton

Shirt number: 10

International team: England

Achievements: 2008 Champions League winner, three-time Premier League champion, two-time PFA Young Player of the Year

Did you know?

Wayne Rooney is England's youngest ever goalscorer. The talented striker found the back of the net against Macedonia in 2003 when he was just 17 years and 317 days old.

Team-mates

Use this space to add some of this player's top team-mates for both club and country.

____

____

____

Scouting Report

Write a list of this player's greatest skills to complete a detailed scouting report.

____

____

____

____

____

Name: Carlos Tevez

The Argentina star is an extremely hardworking footballer, who possesses limitless energy as he hustles and bustles defenders into making mistakes. As well as his industry, Tevez plays with great imagination and creativity, dribbling with speed and skill and finishing with accuracy.

Position: Striker

Born: 5 February, 1984 in Buenos Aires, Argentina

Height: 5 ft 8 in (1.73 m)

Club: Manchester City

Former clubs: Boca Juniors, Corinthians, West Ham United, Manchester United

Shirt number: 32

International team: Argentina

Achievements: 2008 Champions League winner, two-time English Premier League champion, Olympic Gold Medallist

Did you know?

When Tevez signed for Manchester City from Manchester United in 2009, he became the first player to transfer between the two clubs since Terry Cooke made the same move 10 years earlier.

Team-mates

Use this space to add some of this player's top team-mates for both club and country.

______

______

______

Scouting Report

Write a list of this player's greatest skills to complete a detailed scouting report.

______

______

______

______

______

Name: Didier Drogba

Chelsea's lion-hearted striker is a goalscoring powerhouse. Drogba has pace, strength and the composure to find the back of the net under pressure. Good in the air with tight close control and the ability to score from distance, Drogba has been one of the most consistent performers in the Premier League since joining the English giants.

Position: Striker
Born: 11 March, 1978 in Abidjan, Ivory Coast
Height: 6 ft 2 in (1.88 m)
Club: Chelsea
Former clubs: Le Mans, Guingamp, Olympique Marseille
Shirt number: 11
International team: Ivory Coast
Achievements: Three-time FA Premier League champion, three-time FA Cup winner, African Footballer of the Year in 2006 and 2009

Team-mates

Use this space to add some of this player's top team-mates for both club and country.

____

____

____

Did you know?

Didier's uncle was also a professional footballer. He played as a striker for French sides Brest, Dunkerque and Abberville, as well as the Ivory Coast international team.

Scouting Report

Write a list of this player's greatest skills to complete a detailed scouting report.

____

____

____

____

Name: Fernando Torres

Chelsea's extraordinary striker is so important to the Blues. The Spanish international can be a match-winner when he's at the top of his game. Full of pace, energy and craft, Fernando can be lethal when the ball is at his feet.

Position: Striker

Born: 20 March, 1984 in Madrid, Spain

Height: 6 ft 1 in (1.85 m)

Club: Chelsea

Former clubs: Athletico Madrid, Liverpool

Shirt number: 9

International team: Spain

Achievements: 2010 World Cup winner, 2008 European Championship winner, Athletico Madrid's youngest ever captain, aged just 19 years old

Team-mates

Use this space to add some of this player's top team-mates for both club and country.

____

____

____

Did you know?

Fernando's nickname is 'El Nino' which means 'The Kid'.

Scouting Report

Write a list of this player's greatest skills to complete a detailed scouting report.

____

____

____

____

Name: Luis Nani

Nani is beginning to fill the huge boots of Cristiano Ronaldo after his countryman left Old Trafford for Real Madrid in 2009. An exciting talent, able to dribble at pace and take defenders on for fun, Nani can also score spectacular goals from distance and whip in dangerous deliveries from out wide.

Position: Winger
Born: 17 November, 1986 in Praia, Cape Verde
Height: 5 ft 9 in (1.75 m)
Club: Manchester United
Former clubs: Sporting Lisbon
Shirt number: 17
International team: Portugal
Achievements: 2008 Champions League winner, FIFA World Club Cup winner, Portuguese Cup winner

Did you know?

Nani scored during his international debut for Portugal in a 4–2 friendly defeat against Denmark.

Team-mates

Use this space to add some of this player's top team-mates for both club and country.

____

____

____

Scouting Report

Write a list of this player's greatest skills to complete a detailed scouting report.

____

____

____

____

____

Name: Andres Iniesta

One of Spain and Barcelona's midfield magicians, the hugely skilled Iniesta operates in an almost free role, linking up play with intricate passing and incisive through-balls. His first touch is always accurate and his vision helps him create countless chances for team-mates.

Position: Central midfield
Born: 11 May, 1984 in Fuentealbilla, Spain
Height: 5 ft 7 in (1.70 m)
Club: Barcelona
Former clubs: None
Shirt number: 8
International team: Spain
Achievements: 2010 World Cup winner, European Championship winner in 2008, two-time Champions League winner

Team-mates

Use this space to add some of this player's top team-mates for both club and country.

____

____

____

Did you know?

Iniesta played for Spain at Under-16, Under-19 and Under-21 levels before making his full international debut in 2006.

Scouting Report

Write a list of this player's greatest skills to complete a detailed scouting report.

____

____

____

____

____

Name: Rio Ferdinand

The Rolls Royce of defenders, Rio Ferdinand plays with great composure using his natural ability and reading of the game to intercept the ball and start moves from deep.

Position: Defender

Born: 7 November, 1978 in London, England

Height: 6 ft 2 in (1.88 m)

Club: Manchester United

Former clubs: West Ham United, AFC Bournemouth (on loan), Leeds United

Shirt number: 5

International team: England

Achievements: Champions League winner, four-time English Premier League champion, 2008 FIFA World Club Cup winner

Team-mates

Use this space to add some of this player's top team-mates for both club and country.

____

____

____

Did you know?

Rio's brother Anton is also a centre back and plays for Sunderland, whilst his uncle, Les, is a former international striker for England.

Scouting Report

Write a list of this player's greatest skills to complete a detailed scouting report.

Name: Cesc Fàbregas

Arsenal's inspirational creative force, Cesc Fàbregas is a gifted footballer with great vision and technique. The Spanish midfielder often scores crucial and spectacular goals for club and country.

Position: Central midfielder
Born: 4 May, 1987 in Vilassar de Mar, Spain
Height: 5 ft 9 in (1.75 m)
Club: Arsenal
Former clubs: None
Shirt number: 4
International team: Spain
Achievements: 2008 European Championship winner, 2010 World Cup winner, 2005 FA Cup winner with Arsenal

Did you know?

Cesc was named Arsenal club captain in November 2008 and has held onto the armband ever since.

Team-mates

Use this space to add some of this player's top team-mates for both club and country.

____

____

____

Scouting Report

Write a list of this player's greatest skills to complete a detailed scouting report.

____

____

____

____

____

Name: Gareth Bale

Either playing as a left back or winger, Gareth Bale's main asset is his searing pace and ability to dribble past opponents for fun. His left foot is also very powerful and accurate, and his speed is outstanding.

Position: Left back, Winger
Born: 16 July, 1989 in Cardiff, Wales
Height: 6 ft (1.83 m)
Club: Tottenham Hotspur
Former clubs: Southampton
Shirt number: 3
International team: Wales
Achievements: 2009 League Cup finalist, Wales international

Did you know?

Bale became the youngest player to play for Wales. He was just 16 years and 315 days old when he lined up against Trinidad and Tobago in 2006.

Team-mates

Use this space to add some of this player's top team-mates for both club and country.

Scouting Report

Write a list of this player's greatest skills to complete a detailed scouting report.

Name: Joe Hart

A vastly talented young goalkeeper, Joe Hart has already established himself as number one for England and Manchester City, aged just 23 years old. He is a superb shot-stopper with lightning-quick reflexes and bucket loads of confidence.

Position: Goalkeeper

Born: 19 April, 1987 in Shrewsbury, England

Height: 6 ft 5 in (1.95 m)

Club: Manchester City

Former clubs: Shrewsbury Town, Tranmere Rovers (on loan), Blackpool (on loan), Birmingham City (on loan)

Shirt number: 25

International team: England

Achievements: Birmingham City 2009/10 Player of the Year, 2007 League One Play-Off winner, voted the Premier League's best goalkeeper for the 2009/10 season

Did you know?

Joe was named as a substitute for the Shrewsbury Town first team just 15 years old.

Team-mates

Use this space to add some of this player's top team-mates for both club and country.

Scouting Report

Write a list of this player's greatest skills to complete a detailed scouting report.

Name: Kaká

The Brazilian international has everything a good attacking midfielder requires: top technique, great finishing ability and the creative vision to see openings and make things happen.

Position: Attacking midfielder

Born: 22 April, 1982 in Brasilia, Brazil

Height: 6 ft 1 in (1.85 m)

Club: Real Madrid

Former clubs: São Paulo, AC Milan

Shirt number: 8

International team: Brazil

Achievements: 2002 World Cup winner, 2007 European Footballer of the Year, Champions League winner

Did you know?

Kaká was a talented tennis player as a youngster, but decided to concentrate on football when he was offered a contract by São Paulo.

Team-mates

Use this space to add some of this player's top team-mates for both club and country.

Scouting Report

Write a list of this player's greatest skills to complete a detailed scouting report.

Name: Mesut Ozil

Ozil really came to prominence at the 2010 World Cup, where his performances helped inspire Germany to the Semi-finals of the competition. He is a brilliant dribbler who passes with accuracy and can score from range.

Position: Attacking midfielder
Born: 15 October, 1988 in Gelsenkirchen, Germany
Height: 5 ft 11 in (1.81 m)
Club: Real Madrid
Former clubs: Werder Bremen
Shirt number: 23
International team: Germany
Achievements: 2009 UEFA Cup finalist, Bronze medallist for third-place finish at 2010 World Cup, German Cup winner

Did you know?

Mesut started all of Germany's games at the 2010 World Cup and scored a spectacular goal against Ghana in the group stage.

Team-mates

Use this space to add some of this player's top team-mates for both club and country.

Scouting Report

Write a list of this player's greatest skills to complete a detailed scouting report.

EXTRA PROFILES

Use these blank profiles to add any missing players that you think deserve to be in this section.

Name: ______________________________

Position: ______________________________

Born: ______________________________

Height: ______________________________

Club: ______________________________

Former clubs: ______________________________

Shirt number: ______________________________

International team: ______________________________

Achievements: ______________________________

____

Place a player picture here.

Name: ______________________________

Position: ______________________________

Born: ______________________________

Height: ______________________________

Club: ______________________________

Former clubs: ______________________________

Shirt number: ______________________________

International team: ______________________________

Achievements: ______________________________

____

Place a player picture here.

Fill in your own player profile with details about yourself.

Name: ____________________

Date of birth: ____________________

Height: ____________________

Position played: ____________________

Club: ____________________

Shirt number: ____________________

Team supported: ____________________

Country supported: ____________________

Achievements: ____________________

____

Place a picture of yourself here.

Top players are always getting asked about their favourite things during interviews. Fill in the following extra profile info to answer some of the questions that footballers have to field.

Favourite player: ____________________

Favourite stadium: ____________________

Favourite colour: ____________________

Favourite film: ____________________

Favourite TV programme: ____________________

Favourite food: ____________________

Favourite holiday destination: ____________________

MY FOOTBALL TEAM

This section is completely dedicated to your favourite football team. Fill in all the information you know about the team you support and research any stats that you're not sure about to make sure you're one of the most dedicated fans around.

Team name: ______________________

Nickname: ______________________

Team colours: ______________________

Ground: ______________________

Year founded: ______________________

Honours: ______________________

Manager: ______________________

Captain: ______________________

Star players: ______________________

Famous past players: ______________________

____

Favourite eleven:

1. ______________________
2. ______________________
3. ______________________
4. ______________________
5. ______________________
6. ______________________
7. ______________________
8. ______________________
9. ______________________
10. ______________________
11. ______________________

Biggest rivals:

____

____

FAVOURITE MOMENTS

Use this space to add any stickers or pictures showing some of the star players from your favourite team.

Interesting Info

Find out three interesting facts about your team or the current players and write them here.

____

____

____

DREAM TEAM

Use this section to select your dream football team. Pick your favourite current players as well as legends of the game from years gone by.

Formation

Obviously, your team is going to need a goalkeeper. It's a very important position because a good goalkeeper can win you games on his own. Now you need to choose the formation to play in front of your number one. You could go defensive and play three centre backs, or pick an attacking line-up with three strikers. Pick one of the following formations or even have a go at choosing your own. Remember, you can only have 11 players on the pitch!

Draw your chosen formation on the pitch below.

4-4-2
4-3-3
4-2-4
3-5-2
4-1-3-1-1

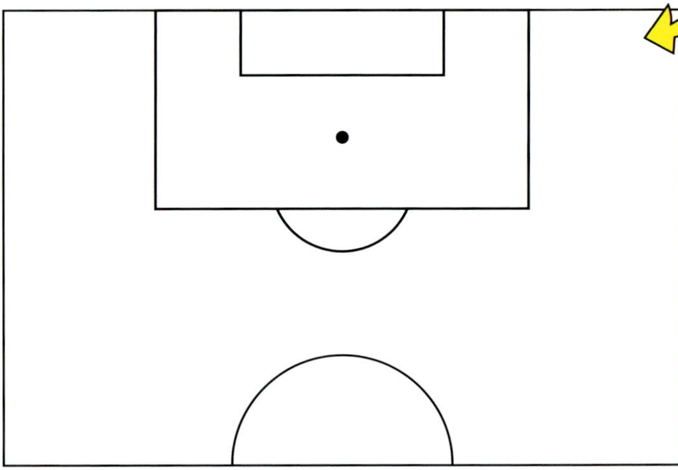

Possible Candidates

If you're stuck for ideas, look through this list of current stars and past legends for inspiration. You can also look back through the Player Profiles section.

Goalkeepers

Current

Edwin van der Sar
Gianluigi Buffon
Iker Casillas
Petr Cech
José Reina

Legends

Peter Schmeichel
Dino Zoff
Gordon Banks
Lev Yashin
Peter Shilton

Right Backs

Current

Maicon
Daniel Alves
Philipp Lahm
Gianluca Zambrotta
Sergio Ramos

Legends

Cafu
Carlos Alberto Torres
Lilian Thuram
Giuseppe Bergomi
Gary Neville

Left Backs

Current

Patrice Evra
Ashley Cole
Gareth Bale
Eric Abidal
Cristian Chivu

Legends

Roberto Carlos
Stuart Pearce
Paolo Maldini
Andreas Brehme
Bixente Lizarazu

Defenders

Current

Nemanja Vidic
Rio Ferdinand
John Terry
Carles Puyol
Gerard Piqué

Legends

Bobby Moore
Franz Beckenbauer
Marcel Desailly
Franco Baresi
Jaap Stam

Midfielders

Current

Xavi Hernandez
Steven Gerrard
Paul Scholes
Wesley Sneijder
Michael Essien

Legends

Zinedine Zidane
Lothar Matthaus
Bobby Charlton
Pavel Nedved
Diego Maradona

Left Wingers

Current

David Silva
Arjen Robben
Lionel Messi
Florent Malouda
Angel Di Maria

Legends

George Best
Ryan Giggs
Marc Overmars
John Barnes
Francisco Gento

Right Wingers

Current

Franck Ribery
Cristiano Ronaldo
Luis Nani
Thomas Muller
Theo Walcott

Legends

Johan Cruyff
Garincha
Stanley Matthews
Luis Figo
David Beckham

Forwards

Current

Wayne Rooney
Carlos Tevez
David Villa
Fernando Torres
Samuel Eto'o

Legends

Pelé
Ferenc Puskas
Gerd Muller
Eric Cantona
Gary Lineker

Team Sheet

Manager: ______________________________

Captain: ______________________________

Now add your team to the team sheet.

1. ______________________________
2. ______________________________
3. ______________________________
4. ______________________________
5. ______________________________
6. ______________________________
7. ______________________________
8. ______________________________
9. ______________________________
10. ______________________________
11. ______________________________

You can name seven substitutes on the bench, so have a think about which players would provide the best back-up for your starting 11 and add them to the list of subs below.

12. ______________________________
13. ______________________________
14. ______________________________
15. ______________________________
16. ______________________________
17. ______________________________
18. ______________________________

FIXTURES & RESULTS LIST

Use these pages to keep track of how your favourite teams are doing and plan ahead to make sure you don't miss some of the biggest games of the season.

Date	Kick-Off	Venue	Team	Opponents

Jot down the games for the team you support, the teams you play for and when your favourite players are going to be in action.

Date	Kick-Off	Venue	Team	Opponents

Place a picture of your team here.

SQUAD LISTS

Check out the following pages to find out the vital statistics of some of Europe's biggest clubs. There will be facts about the stadiums, managers and the players. Then complete the blank contact details sections, adding names, addresses, numbers and email addresses of your friends and family.

Team Sheet

Fill in the team sheet for each of the top teams. Fill in as many players as you know in each position that play for the club, and maybe add a few of your dream signings. Manchester United's team sheet has been started for you.

Manchester United

Nickname: The Red Devils
Stadium: Old Trafford
Capacity: 76,212
Manager: Sir Alex Ferguson
Captain: Nemanja Vidic

Goalkeepers
Edwin van der Sar
____
____

Defenders
____
____
Rio Ferdinand
Nemanja Vidic
____
____
____

Midfielders
Darren Fletcher
Ryan Giggs
____
Ji-Sung Park
____
____
Luis Nani

Forwards
Wayne Rooney
Javier Hernandez
____
____
Federico Macheda
____
____

Team Sheet

Chelsea

Nickname: The Blues
Stadium: Stamford Bridge
Capacity: 41,841
Manager: Carlo Ancelotti
Captain: John Terry

Place a team or player picture here.

Goalkeepers

____
____
____

Defenders

____
____
____
____
____
____
____

Midfielders

____
____
____
____
____
____
____

Forwards

____
____
____
____
____
____
____
____

Contacts

Name: ______________________
Address: ______________________
____
Telephone: ______________________
Email: ______________________

Team Sheet

Arsenal

Nickname: The Gunners
Stadium: The Emirates Stadium
Capacity: 60,335
Manager: Arsene Wenger
Captain: Cesc Fàbregas

Place a team or player picture here.

Goalkeepers

Defenders

Midfielders

Forwards

Contacts

Name:

Address:

Telephone:

Email:

Contacts

Name: ____________________

Address: ____________________

____

Telephone: ____________________

Email: ____________________

Team Sheet

Liverpool

Nickname: The Reds
Stadium: Anfield
Capacity: 45,362
Manager: Kenny Dalglish
Captain: Steven Gerrard

Goalkeepers

____
____
____

Defenders

____
____
____
____
____
____
____

Midfielders

____
____

Place a team or player picture here.

____
____
____
____
____
____

Forwards

____
____
____
____
____
____
____
____

Team Sheet

Manchester City

Nickname: The Blues, The Citizens
Stadium: The City of Manchester Stadium
Capacity: 47,726
Manager: Roberto Mancini
Captain: Carlos Tevez

Place a team or player picture here.

Goalkeepers

____
____
____

Defenders

____
____
____
____
____
____
____

Midfielders

____
____
____
____
____
____
____
____

Forwards

____
____
____
____
____
____
____
____

Contacts

Name: ____________________
Address: ____________________
____
Telephone: ____________________
Email: ____________________

Contacts

Name: ____________________

Address: ____________________

____

Telephone: ____________________

Email: ____________________

Team Sheet

Tottenham Hotspur

Nickname: Spurs
Stadium: White Hart Lane
Capacity: 36,310
Manager: Harry Redknapp
Captain: Ledley King

Place a team or player picture here.

Goalkeepers

Defenders

Midfielders

Forwards

Team Sheet

Barcelona

Nickname: Barca
Stadium: Nou Camp
Capacity: 98,800
Manager: Josep Guardiola
Captain: Carles Puyol

Place a team or player picture here.

Goalkeepers

____
____
____

Defenders

____
____
____
____
____
____
____

Midfielders

____
____
____
____
____
____
____
____

Forwards

____
____
____
____
____
____
____
____

Contacts

Name: ________________________
Address: ________________________
____
Telephone: ________________________
Email: ________________________

Contacts

Name: ____________________

Address: ____________________

____

Telephone: ____________________

Email: ____________________

Team Sheet

Real Madrid

Nickname: The Whites

Stadium: Santiago Bernabeu Stadium

Capacity: 80,354

Manager: José Mourinho

Captain: Iker Casillas

Place a team or player picture here.

Goalkeepers

____

____

____

Defenders

____

____

____

____

____

____

____

Midfielders

____

____

____

____

____

____

____

____

Forwards

____

____

____

____

____

____

____

____

Team Sheet

AC Milan

Nickname: The Rossoneri
Stadium: San Siro
Capacity: 85,700
Manager: Massimiliano Allegri
Captain: Massimo Ambrosini

Place a team or player picture here.

Goalkeepers

____
____
____

Defenders

____
____
____
____
____
____
____

Midfielders

____
____
____
____
____
____
____
____

Forwards

____
____
____
____
____
____
____
____

Contacts

Name: ____________________
Address: ____________________
____
Telephone: ____________________
Email: ____________________

Contacts

Name: ______________________________

Address: ______________________________

____

Telephone: ______________________________

Email: ______________________________

Team Sheet

Bayern Munich

Nickname: The Bavarians, The Reds
Stadium: Allianz Arena
Capacity: 66,901
Manager: Luis van Gaal
Captain: Mark van Bommel

Place a team or player picture here.

Goalkeepers

____
____
____

Defenders

____
____
____
____
____
____
____

Midfielders

____
____
____
____
____
____
____
____

Forwards

____
____
____
____
____
____
____
____

Team Sheet

Juventus

Nickname: Juve, The Old Lady
Stadium: Stadio Olimpico di Torino
Capacity: 28,000
Manager: Luigi Delneri
Captain: Alessandro Del Piero

Place a team or player picture here.

Goalkeepers

Defenders

Midfielders

Forwards

Contacts

Name:

Address:

Telephone:

Email:

Now fill in these blank profiles of any teams that haven't been included in this section.

Contacts

Name: ____________________

Address: ____________________

____

Telephone: ____________________

Email: ____________________

Team: ____________________

Nickname: ____________________

Stadium: ____________________

Capacity: ____________________

Manager: ____________________

Captain: ____________________

Star player: ____________________

Place a picture of your chosen team here.

Contacts

Name: ____________________

Address: ____________________

____

Telephone: ____________________

Email: ____________________

Contacts

Name: ____________________

Address: ____________________

____

Telephone: ____________________

Email: ____________________

Team: ____________________

Nickname: ____________________

Stadium: ____________________

Capacity: ____________________

Manager: ____________________

Captain: ____________________

Star player: ____________________

Place a picture of your chosen team here.

Contacts

Name: ____________________

Address: ____________________

____

Telephone: ____________________

Email: ____________________

Contacts

Name: ____________________

Address: ____________________

____

Telephone: ____________________

Email: ____________________

Team: ____________________

Nickname: ____________________

Stadium: ____________________

Capacity: ____________________

Manager: ____________________

Captain: ____________________

Star player: ____________________

Place a picture of your chosen team here.

Contacts

Name: ____________________

Address: ____________________

____

Telephone: ____________________

Email: ____________________

FITNESS FILE

This section provides fitness information, pre-match food ideas and top tips on skills and techniques to help you improve your footy talent and prepare properly for training and matches.

Skills & Techniques

Check out these quick tips for ideas of how to improve different football skills.

First Touch

Your first touch of the ball is vital to getting it under control and keeping possession for your team. Next time you're watching your favourite players, concentrate on their first touch.

Cushioning the Ball

To cushion the ball, make sure that your body is relaxed to help you take the power out of the pass or cross. Then, make sure your body position allows you to be well balanced and able to receive the ball.

A player with a great first touch: ______________________________

Striking the Ball

When taking a shot or making a long pass or clearance with power, it is important to keep your eye on the ball and make sure your head and body are leaning over it.

A player who strikes the ball with good technique and power:

____

Hitting a Volley

When volleying the ball, sticking your arms out for balance can help you control the rest of your body. Make sure you watch the ball right onto your foot too, and don't swing your leg too early.

A player who is renowned for his volleys:

____

Passing the Ball

When passing the ball, think about how your team-mate wants to receive it. Make it as easy as possible by being accurate and using the right power and height on your delivery.

A player who is a great passer of the ball:

____

Keeping Shots on Target

Try to keep your knee over the ball and your head down as this will help keep your body and your shot down. Think about which foot you should strike the ball with too. It won't always bounce perfectly on your strongest foot, so don't be afraid to take a shot with your other foot.

An accurate finisher in front of goal: ______________________

Successful Dribbling

Don't let the ball get too far ahead of you. Even when you want to run faster, a heavy touch could give the defender a chance to tackle you.

A skilful dribbler: ______________________

Tackling

Try to stay on your feet as much as possible to make block tackles and interceptions. A slide tackle can be an effective way of winning back possession for your team, but it should only be used as a last resort.

A top tackler: ______________________

Pre-Match Meal Ideas

Think about when you're playing, whether it's in the morning, afternoon or evening, and plan ahead to decide when and what is best to eat. Write down your pre-match meal ideas.

Breakfast: ______________________________

____

Light lunch: ______________________________

____

Evening meal: ______________________________

____

Drinks

Drink as much fluid as possible, but think about what would be best for you.

____

____

Snacks

A good snack to eat before a game is a banana because they are full of carbohydrates which convert into energy. Think about some other options.

____

____

SUPERSTAR
SUPERSTAR
SUPERSTAR
SUPERSTAR

AON

Fly Emirates

SAMSUNG

WINNERS

MAN OF THE MATC

GOAL KICK

BEAT THE WALL

TOP TACKLE

BACK OF THE NET

STAR PLAYER

LEGEND

SUPERSTAR

Fitness Plan

You've had some pre-match meal advice and training tips, now plan your own fitness regime to get into peak fitness for your next match.

Think about what type of exercise or football practice you can do and when you'll be able to do it. Then write down a routine, jotting down times and dates for the next few weeks and try to keep to it.

Some examples of things you should be thinking about include going for a run, practising passing and control, either with friends or on your own by kicking the ball against a wall, and ways of warming up and warming down before and after exercise.

Day: ____________________

Time: ____________________

Activity: ____________________

Location: ____________________

Eating and drinking plan: ____________________

SCRAPBOOK

Use this section to fill in your own footy facts and trivia, stick in your favourite stickers, add newspaper and magazine cuttings and photos.

Use this space to write about the best goal you have ever scored.

____

____

____

____

Trivia

Italy and AC Milan legend Paolo Maldini is the only man to have played in a Champions League Final in three different decades.

Did you know?

Sol Campbell and Ryan Giggs are the only two players to have played in every Premier League season since the league started in 1992. Giggs is the only man to have scored in every single Premier League season.

Fill in the following details of the first game you ever saw live.

Ground: ______________________________

Teams playing: ______________________________

Score: ______________________________

Goalscorers: ______________________________

Did you know?

Manchester United created a Premier League goalscoring record when they beat Ipswich Town 9–0 in 1995. It remains the league's biggest winning margin, but Spurs got close in 2010 when they beat Wigan Athletic 9–1.

Trivia

Manchester United striker Dimitar Berbatov claims to have learned to speak English by watching all three Godfather films.

Jot down three young players that you think are going to develop into international stars in the future.

1. ______________________________

2. ______________________________

3. ______________________________

Use this space to add any footy pictures, stickers or clippings.

Did you know?

A total of £87m in transfer fees has been spent on Chelsea striker Nicolas Anelka throughout his career!

Trivia

In 2002, Turkey striker Hakan Sukur scored the fastest ever World Cup goal when he netted after just 11 seconds in the third-place play-off against South Korea.

Use your footy knowledge to fill in the following factsheet.

2010 World Cup winners: ______

Manchester United's manager: ______

Arsenal's home ground: ______

2009/10 Premier League winners: ______

England's manager: ______

Name three Italian teams: ______

Name two Spanish teams: ______

Name one German team: ______

Trivia

UEFA President Michel Platini lifted the 1980 European Championships as captain of France. Les Bleus beat Spain in the Final and Platini scored nine of France's 14 goals as they progressed through the tournament.

Use this space to add any footy pictures, stickers or clippings.

Did you know?

Steven Gerrard made his 500th club appearance for Liverpool against Blackburn Rovers at Ewood Park on 12 December, 2009.

Write down the names of as many tricks and flicks as you can in this box. One example is the 'stepover'.

Use this space to add any footy pictures, stickers or clippings.

Did you know?

In a friendly match against France in Paris on 26 March 2008, David Beckham became only the fifth Englishman to win 100 international caps.

Trivia

Bobby Charlton is England's all-time leading goalscorer. The Manchester United legend scored an impressive 49 goals in 106 international appearances.

A-Z OF FOOTBALL TRIVIA

A

AC Milan Appearances

AC Milan legend Paolo Maldini holds the record for the most number of appearances for Milan, with a total of 1,000 games played, including 600 in Serie A. Maldini's number 3 shirt has been retired by the San Siro giants as a mark of respect for his achievements and long service to the club.

B

Brilliant Barca

In 2009, Barcelona became the first Spanish club to win a treble of the La Liga championship, the Spanish Cup and the UEFA Champions League.

C

Cruyff Turn

The Cruyff Turn is a piece of top quality skill named after the legendary Ajax, Barcelona and Holland star, Johan Cruyff, who first developed the turn. The trick involves shaping your body one way to give the impression you are going to cross or clear the ball, before quickly cutting the ball back along the ground behind you to beat your marker.

D

David Did It

David Beckham became the first English player to score in three separate World Cups when he scored a free kick against Ecuador in a second-round match at the 2006 World Cup.

E

Eric's Off

Manchester United legend Eric Cantona was sent off twice in four days whilst playing for the Red Devils in the Premier League in 1994.

F

Fergie Time

Sir Alex Ferguson officially became Manchester United's longest-serving manager on 19 December, 2010, when his 24 years in charge as United boss overtook the previous record set by another Reds legend, Sir Matt Busby.

G

Gudjohnsens

Former Chelsea forward Eidur Gudjohnsen, now at Stoke City, once replaced his dad as a substitute during an international match for Iceland.

H

Howard's Honour

Goalkeeper Tim Howard became the first American to win an FA Cup winners medal when he played in goal for Manchester United against Millwall in the 2004 Final.

Invincibles

When Arsenal won the 2003/04 Premier League title, they didn't lose a single game. The Gunners were unbeaten in 38 league games and became labelled 'The Invincibles'.

Juventus

The Italian giants currently hold the record for the most Serie A titles, with an impressive 27 first-place finishes.

Kicking Klinsmann

Legendary German striker Jurgen Klinsmann scored in every single one of the six major international tournaments he played in, from Euro 1988 to the 1998 World Cup. During that time, he lifted the 1990 World Cup and the 1996 European Championship.

Place a picture here.

Place a picture here.

Liverpool Legend

Liverpool's all-time leading scorer in all competitions is Welsh striker Ian Rush, who scored 346 goals in his two spells at the club from 1980 to 1987 and 1988 to 1996.

M

Manchester United

Manchester United were founded as Newton Heath in 1878. The club changed its name to Manchester United in 1902 and moved to Old Trafford in 1910.

N

Nevilles

Former England internationals Gary and Phil Neville's dad is called Neville Neville.

O

Oliver 'King' Khan

Former German goalkeeper Oliver Kahn is the only stopper in the history of the game to have won the FIFA World Cup Golden Ball – the award for the best player of the World Cup. Kahn earned the trophy after taking Germany to the Final of the 2002 tournament.

Place a picture here.

P

Pressman Walks

Former Sheffield Wednesday goalkeeper Kevin Pressman holds the record for the fastest ever red card in English football. He was sent off after just 13 seconds on the opening day of the 2000/01 season against Wolves.

Q

Quids In

When Real Madrid signed Cristiano Ronaldo from Manchester United in 2009, they paid the English club a world record £80m.

R

Ronaldo's Record

During the 2006 FIFA World Cup, Brazil striker Ronaldo became the highest goalscorer in World Cup history when he netted his 15th goal in the tournament, overtaking Gerd Muller's previous record of 14.

S

Shearer Scores

Former England striker Alan Shearer holds the record for the most goals scored in Premier League history. 'Big Al' bagged an impressive 260 goals for Blackburn Rovers and Newcastle United.

T

Tottenham's Time

When the year ends with one, it's speculated that Tottenham Hotspur are likely to win a trophy. The North London club won the English First Division in 1951, a league and cup double in 1961 and the FA Cup in 1981 and 1991.

Place a picture here.

U

Uruguay

Uruguay was the first country to win the World Cup. The South Americans beat Argentina 4–2 in the Final of the 1930 tournament, which was held on home soil.

V

Van the Man

In January 2009, Manchester United goalkeeper Edwin van der Sar helped the club set a new Premier League record for the number of consecutive clean sheets. A 5–0 win over West Bromwich Albion meant that United had gone 11 games and 1,032 minutes without conceding a goal.

W

Wembley

The arch at the new Wembley Stadium weighs as much as ten jumbo jets.

X

X-ray

After a nasty collision with a Birmingham City forward in the 1956 FA Cup Final, Manchester City goalkeeper Bert Trautmann stayed on and played the last 15 minutes of the game. His team won 3–1, but three days later an X-ray revealed that Bert had actually broken his neck!

Y

Yellow Card Crazy

English referee Graham Poll infamously issued three yellow cards to Croatia defender Josip Simunic in one match before he had to send him off at the 2006 World Cup.

Z

Zinedine Zidane

French legend Zinedine Zidane received a red card in the 2006 World Cup Final, his last ever game in professional football. It was the 14th sending off of 'Zizou's' career.

Place a picture here.

ACTIVITIES

You've read top footy facts and trivia so far on some of the world's best players. Now complete these action-packed puzzles and activities and see how good your football knowledge is. Are you the ultimate football fan or will you need some extra training?

TRUE OR FALSE?

Work out if the statements about the teams and players from the English Premier League are true or false.

1. Liverpool have not won the Premier League title since the league changed from the Old First Division in 1992. ____________

2. Ryan Giggs has only ever played for Manchester United in the Premier League. ____________

3. Chelsea and Arsenal both play their home games in Birmingham. ____________

4. Arsene Wenger is the manager of Arsenal. ____________

5. Alan Shearer's former clubs include Tottenham Hotspur and Manchester City. ____________

6. Cristiano Ronaldo used to play in the Premier League for Bolton Wanderers. ____________

7. Everton play their home games at Goodison Park. ____________

8. Newcastle United's home kit is made up of black and white stripes. ____________

9. Chelsea won the Premier League title in 2010. ____________

10. The first ever winners of the Premier League were Blackburn Rovers. ____________

11. Aston Villa have played in every single Premier League season so far. ____________

12. Steven Gerrard is captain of Liverpool. ____________

SPOT THE BALL

Check out these two action photographs. Everything looks normal except that the ball is missing! Use two of your football stickers to mark where you think the ball should be in each picture.

Grid 2

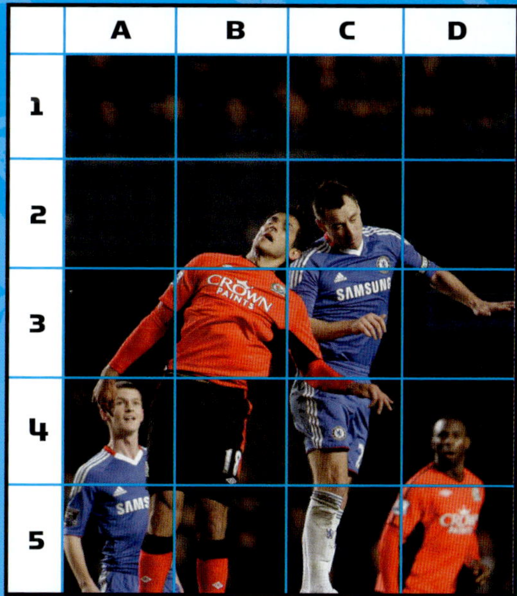

Grid 1

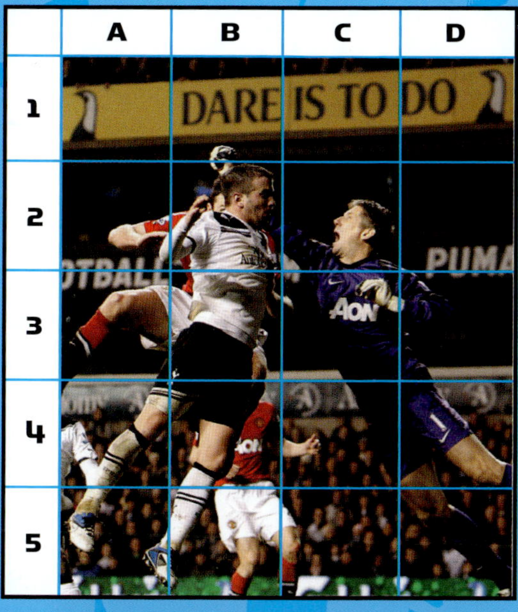

FOOTBALL WORDSEARCH

Check through this wordsearch to find all 15 of the footy-themed words. The words will be written forwards, backwards, horizontally, vertically and diagonally.

Q	P	E	N	A	L	T	Y	K	E
U	L	L	A	B	T	S	D	L	E
C	O	R	N	E	R	V	B	H	D
T	R	S	H	O	T	B	T	E	I
E	E	R	G	B	I	S	E	A	S
N	F	J	H	R	O	J	V	D	F
K	E	P	D	P	V	M	A	E	F
I	R	Z	A	T	I	X	S	R	O
C	E	D	O	S	F	D	I	V	E
K	E	N	F	L	S	L	A	O	G

ball	dive	penalty
net	goal	shot
header	corner	pass
referee	kick	dribble
post	offside	save

TEAM ANAGRAMS

These famous club sides have been jumbled up. Can you sort the letters to reveal the correct club?

1. SLANERA ______________________

2. CA NLIAM ______________________

3. RACELOBNA ______________________

4. FINCABE ______________________

5. HEAMNCSTER NIDTUE ______________________

6. STEVUNJU ______________________

7. ALER DRAMDI ______________________

8. SEECHAL ______________________

9. CHILETOTA RADDIM ______________________

10. YABREN CHUMIN ______________________

11. POLORIVEL ______________________

12. RINET LAMIN ______________________

WHO AM I?

For each question there will be three clues describing one of the most famous footballers in the world. Can you guess which player is being described for each one?

1. My nickname is Wazza, I play up front for Manchester United and England, and I usually wear the number 10 shirt. ____________________

2. I was part of Spain's World Cup-winning team, I play up front for Barcelona and my initials are D.V. ____________________

3. I play international football for Argentina, my club side is Barcelona, where I play as a winger, and I won the Champions League in 2009. ____________________

4. I joined my current team, Real Madrid, from Manchester United, I wear the number seven shirt and I'm a free-kick specialist. ____________________

5. I am a Brazilian international, I play as an attacking midfielder and my current club is Real Madrid. ____________________

6. I play up front for the Blues from Stamford Bridge, I used to play for Marseille and I am captain of the Ivory Coast international team. ____________________

7. I am Liverpool captain, I play in midfield for England and I scored in the 2005 Champions League Final. ____________________

8. I famously moved from Manchester United to Manchester City, I play as a striker and my initials are C.T. ____________________

9. I am the youngest player to have made an international appearance for England, I play on the wing for the Gunners and I used to play for Southampton. ____________________

10. I am a Cameroon international, I've won the Champions League three times and my first name is Samuel. ____________________

COUNTRY MATCH

Check out the list of players on the left and the list of countries on the right. Work out which nation the player has played for, draw a line to match their name to the country and add the correct flag sticker.

1. Guiseppe Rossi	**Cameroon**
2. Steven Gerrard	**Portugal**
3. Mesut Ozil	**Argentina**
4. Carlos Tevez	**Brazil**
5. Robinho	**Serbia**
6. Gareth Bale	**England**
7. Wesley Sneijder	**Germany**
8. Samuel Eto'o	**Netherlands**
9. Luis Nani	**Italy**
10. Nemanja Vidic	**Wales**

ANSWERS

Page 62

1. True
2. True
3. False
4. True
5. False
6. False
7. True
8. True
9. True
10. False
11. True
12. True

Page 63

Grid 1: A1
Grid 2: B1

Page 64

Q	P	E	N	A	L	T	Y	K	E
U	L	L	A	B	T	S	D	L	E
C	O	R	N	E	R	V	B	H	D
T	R	S	H	O	T	B	T	E	I
E	E	R	G	B	I	S	E	A	S
N	F	J	H	R	O	J	V	D	F
K	E	R	D	P	V	M	A	E	F
I	R	Z	A	T	I	X	S	R	O
C	E	D	O	S	F	D	I	V	E
K	E	N	F	L	S	L	A	O	G

Page 65

1. ARSENAL
2. AC MILAN
3. BARCELONA
4. BENFICA
5. MANCHESTER UNITED
6. JUVENTUS
7. REAL MADRID
8. CHELSEA
9. ATHLETICO MADRID
10. BAYERN MUNICH
11. LIVERPOOL
12. INTER MILAN

Page 66

1. Wayne Rooney
2. David Villa
3. Lionel Messi
4. Cristiano Ronaldo
5. Kaká
6. Didier Drogba
7. Steven Gerrard
8. Carlos Tevez
9. Theo Walcott
10. Samuel Eto'o

Page 67

1. Guiseppe Rossi	Italy
2. Steven Gerrard	England
3. Mesut Ozil	Germany
4. Carlos Tevez	Argentina
5. Robinho	Brazil
6. Gareth Bale	Wales
7. Wesley Sneijder	Netherlands
8. Samuel Eto'o	Cameroon
9. Luis Nani	Portugal
10. Nemanja Vidic	Serbia

CALENDAR

Use this calendar to plan the weeks and months ahead, making sure you never miss an important date or footy game again. Add the birthdays of your friends, family and favourite players, and keep a check of when you've got matches for your club and school teams, or just jot down the days you're going to be having a kick around with your mates. You can also check out cool footy facts throughout the calendar.

MONTH/YEAR ____________________

MON	TUE
WED	THU

FRI	SAT	SUN

Lionel Messi has been named the Argentine Player of the Year on four occasions, in 2005, 2007, 2008 and 2009.

MON	TUE
WED	THU

FRI	SAT	SUN

My favourite game ever: ____________________

MONTH/YEAR ______________________

When England played Malta at Wembley in 1971, the match was so one-sided that the ball didn't cross the England goal-line once in the entire 90 minutes.

MON ☐	TUE ☐
WED ☐	THU ☐

FRI ☐	SAT ☐	SUN ☐

MON ☐	TUE ☐
WED ☐	THU ☐

FRI ☐	SAT ☐	SUN ☐

MONTH/YEAR ____________________

MON	TUE
WED	THU

FRI	SAT	SUN

Chelsea striker Didier Drogba was named African Player of the Year for the second time in 2009.

MON	TUE
WED	THU

FRI	SAT	SUN

Best team I've played for: ____________________

MONTH/YEAR ____________________

MON	TUE
WED	THU

FRI	SAT	SUN

MON	TUE
WED	THU

FRI	SAT	SUN

Oleg Salenko scored five goals for Russia when they beat Cameroon 6–1 in the 1994 World Cup in the United States. It remains the most goals that any player has scored in a single World Cup match.

MONTH/YEAR ____________________

MON	TUE
WED	THU

FRI	SAT	SUN

Cristiano Ronaldo was the first ever Portuguese player to play for Manchester United.

MON	TUE
WED	THU

FRI	SAT	SUN

Best team I've played against: ____________________

MONTH/YEAR ____________________

MON	TUE
WED	THU

FRI	SAT	SUN

When Spain won the 2010 World Cup in South Africa, they became the first European country to win the tournament in a different continent.

MON	TUE
WED	THU

FRI	SAT	SUN

MONTH/YEAR ______

German legend Lothar Matthaus holds the record for most World Cup appearances. The World Cup winner played in 25 games between 1982 and 1998.

MON ☐	TUE ☐	
WED ☐	THU ☐	
FRI ☐	SAT ☐	SUN ☐
MON ☐	TUE ☐	
WED ☐	THU ☐	
FRI ☐	SAT ☐	SUN ☐

The opposition player I would love to have play for my team:

______

MONTH/YEAR ______________________________

MON	TUE
WED	THU

FRI	SAT	SUN

Thierry Henry is Arsenal's record goalscorer. The former France international bagged an impressive 226 goals in just 380 games.

MON	TUE
WED	THU

FRI	SAT	SUN

MONTH/YEAR ______________________

MON	TUE
WED	THU

FRI	SAT	SUN

Former England goalkeeper Peter Shilton made 1,005 competitive appearances in the English Football League, which remains a record.

MON	TUE
WED	THU

FRI	SAT	SUN

My favourite manager: ______________________

MONTH/YEAR ______________________

MON	TUE
WED	THU

FRI	SAT	SUN

MON	TUE
WED	THU

FRI	SAT	SUN

There is estimated to be at least 333 million Manchester United fans around the world. They would fill Old Trafford 4,380 times over!

MONTH/YEAR ____________________

Nottingham Forest are the only club to have won the European Cup more times (twice) than they have won their domestic league (once).

MON ☐	TUE ☐
WED ☐	THU ☐

FRI ☐	SAT ☐	SUN ☐

MON ☐	TUE ☐
WED ☐	THU ☐

FRI ☐	SAT ☐	SUN ☐

A top-class referee that I know: ____________________

MONTH/YEAR ____________________

MON	TUE
WED	THU

FRI	SAT	SUN

MON	TUE
WED	THU

FRI	SAT	SUN

In 1963, legendary Russian stopper Lev Yashin became the only goalkeeper to win the European Footballer of the Year Award.

MONTH/YEAR ______________________

MON	TUE
WED	THU

FRI	SAT	SUN

During the 2007/2008 season, Cristiano Ronaldo scored an impressive 35 goals in 37 domestic and European matches. The winger's goals helped Manchester United win the Premier League and the Champions League that season.

MON	TUE
WED	THU

FRI	SAT	SUN

Best football stadium I've been to: ______________________

MONTH/YEAR

Carlos Tevez was sent off twice in three international games whilst playing for Argentina. He was red carded against Colombia and Paraguay during the South American's World Cup qualifying campaign.

MON	TUE
WED	THU

FRI	SAT	SUN

MON	TUE
WED	THU

FRI	SAT	SUN

MONTH/YEAR ____________________

MON	TUE
WED	THU

FRI	SAT	SUN

During his time at Manchester United, Ruud van Nistelrooy scored an impressive six hat-tricks.

MON	TUE
WED	THU

FRI	SAT	SUN

My favourite goalkeeper: ____________________

MONTH/YEAR ____________________

Francesco Totti is Roma's record goalscorer and the most capped player in the club's history.

MON ☐ | TUE ☐

WED ☐ | THU ☐

FRI ☐ | SAT ☐ | SUN ☐

MON ☐ | TUE ☐

WED ☐ | THU ☐

FRI ☐ | SAT ☐ | SUN ☐

MONTH/YEAR ____________

MON	TUE
WED	THU

FRI	SAT	SUN

Aston Villa goalkeeper Brad Friedel holds the record for the number of consecutive Premier League appearances. The American stopper played 241 games in a row.

MON	TUE
WED	THU

FRI	SAT	SUN

My favourite defender: ____________

MONTH/YEAR ____________________

MON	TUE
WED	THU

FRI	SAT	SUN

David Trezeguet is the highest-scoring foreign player in Juventus' history.

MON	TUE
WED	THU

FRI	SAT	SUN

MONTH/YEAR ______________________

MON ☐	TUE ☐
WED ☐	THU ☐

FRI ☐	SAT ☐	SUN ☐

Blackburn Rovers became the first team to score seven goals in a Premier League game when they beat Norwich City in 1992.

MON ☐	TUE ☐
WED ☐	THU ☐

FRI ☐	SAT ☐	SUN ☐

My favourite midfielder: ______________________

MONTH/YEAR ____________________

MON	TUE
WED	THU

FRI	SAT	SUN

MON	TUE
WED	THU

FRI	SAT	SUN

Six host nations have won the World Cup on home soil, including England in 1966.

MONTH/YEAR ______________________

MON ☐	TUE ☐
WED ☐	THU ☐

FRI ☐	SAT ☐	SUN ☐

The biggest ever attendance in a World Cup match came in the 1986 Final between Argentina and West Germany. 114,600 people packed into the Estadio Azteca in Mexico to watch the game.

MON ☐	TUE ☐
WED ☐	THU ☐

FRI ☐	SAT ☐	SUN ☐

My favourite striker: ______________________

MONTH/YEAR ____________________

MON	TUE

WED	THU

FRI	SAT	SUN

MON	TUE

WED	THU

FRI	SAT	SUN

Celtic became the first British side to win the European Cup in 1967.

MONTH/YEAR ____________________

MON	TUE
WED	THU

FRI	SAT	SUN

Blackburn Rovers goalkeeper Paul Robinson has scored twice so far in his career. One was a header for his old club Leeds United and the second came from a free kick from inside his own half that bounced over Paul's former England team-mate, Ben Foster.

MON	TUE
WED	THU

FRI	SAT	SUN

MONTH/YEAR ____________________

When Cameroon's Roger Milla scored a consolation goal for the Indomitable Lions in a 6–1 trouncing by Russia in 1994, he became the oldest goalscorer in World Cup history at 42 years and 39 days old.

MON ☐	TUE ☐
WED ☐	THU ☐

FRI ☐	SAT ☐	SUN ☐

MON ☐	TUE ☐
WED ☐	THU ☐

FRI ☐	SAT ☐	SUN ☐